GW00578946

A FAMILY BEHIND GLASS

Matthew Hedley Stoppard was born in Derbyshire in 1985. After a brief career as a journalist, he now works at Headingley Library, and lives in Leeds with his wife and two sons.

Recordings of Matthew's poetry include *Insect Eucharist and Other Poems* (2012) and the spoken-word album *Runt Country* (2014), both available from Adult Teeth Recordings. On the page, his poetry has appeared in *Magma, Iota, Cake, The Morning Star, A Complicated Way of Being Ignored* (Grist, 2012) and *Holding Your Hand Through Hard Times* (Osset Originals, 2014). This is his first collection.

A Family
Behind Glass

M<small>ATTHEW</small> H<small>EDLEY</small>
S<small>TOPPARD</small>

VP

Valley Press

First published in 2013 by Valley Press
Woodend, The Crescent, Scarborough, YO11 2PW
www.valleypressuk.com

First edition, second printing (February 2015)

ISBN 978-1-908853-20-2
Cat. no. VP0044

Printed and bound in Great Britain by
Imprint Digital, Upton Pyne, Exeter

www.valleypressuk.com/authors/matthewhedleystoppard

Contents

Acknowledgements

I would like to thank the editors of the following publications, anthologies and websites, where some of these poems have previously appeared: *The Cadaverine, Cake, A Complicated Way of Being Ignored* (Grist), *Dead Ink, First Time, Gammag, Iota, The Morning Star* and *The Ugly Tree*.

Unfathomable thanks to Jimmy Andrex, Pete Bunten, John Irving Clarke, Gareth Durasow, Rob Hudson, Jamie McGarry, Harriet Tarlo and Nigel Whittaker.

Dedicated to the mothers, sisters and father.

A Family Behind Glass

When I sprouted legs

Sunday school doors swung open;
honest as hymns, I was first out
into fields necklaced with pylons,
still reciting the Lord's Prayer,
brushing biscuit crumbs
from my Ladybird waistcoat.

Within hiccups the pondside
appeared and I nestled in
the ribbet and bulrushes
every inch of my skin ticklish,
dazzled by bright browns
my eyes turned into tadpoles,
fixated on tectonic lilypads,
and I gave confession
to the priestly mallard.

Heron-headed drinkers,
grey hair fine and side-parted,
spoke psalmfully with their
thees and thines
remarking on the toy hearse
I pushed under snooker tables
and dartboards and the time
a mix of shandy and sherbert
foamed me rabid.

Swept up in sugar and fizz
wallpaper surrounded me;
reassured by tumbledried clothes

the hum of hoovers lulled
and someone put a lampshade
on my sun. Digits become fingers,
calcium spots orbiting
the nail's quick fade –
I have signed
my tenancy with manhood
but I'll ribbet before I croak.

Half day fairy tale

Whilst listening to him whistling like a spaghetti western
she absentmindedly ate the label on her apple.
His lips unlooped to say:
   'What time's your mother expecting you home?'
Birthday cake for breakfast had made her stomach turn;
sat beneath four balloons tied to a dining table,
hoping to float away
   and not have to say goodbye on the platform.

Seagulls squealed above Birmingham New Street
like wheels gathering speed on a rusty bicycle.
She nibbled the pips from the apple core and replied:
   'Before one.'
Sable curlicues escaped her hair grips and tickled
his nose as he genuflected to envelop her –
she thought of horses nuzzling, affectionately wrapping
   their heads around each others'.

Meanwhile he cursed the clown that wouldn't perform
in the morning, the novelty candles that didn't re-ignite
when extinguished, and, most of all, Midlands Mainline.
   'It's the cold making my eyes cry,'
he whimpered once her carriage was dragged northwards.
Unable to hold her crayons steady, and stay inside
the line of her colouring book, when the train swayed,
   she looked out of the window and into a fridge:

margarine tub bungalows stood before a forest
of broccoli florets and the fields were laid out
like lettuce leaves. Remembering her bellyache she scribbled:

'Would a seed planted in Victoria sponge
grow into a Granny Smiths tree?' She would save this question
for him and brought her legs up under her chin in a huddle.
It was dark. Either someone had closed the fridge door
   or the train had entered a tunnel.

Kimberley could sing

Her parents turned away for the first time
as Kimberley sat with her legs dangling
    like treasury tags between spindles on the stairs
        leading backstage.

Knotted hair
and shoelaces, tonsils already removed,
    boys' hearts took residence in Monopoly hotels
        spilling from her dungaree pocket.

Her parents turned away for the second time,
beckoning the fish-man and his basket swimming
    with pickled cockles and rubbery mussels.

The local covers vocalist hit a high note and Kimberley
stopped slurping Dandelion and Burdock through five
    straws;
    started lip-syncing at the landlord.

Her parents turned away for the last time,
perfecting perms and detecting friends' aftershaves
    further down the buttonback leather bench.

Kimberley found an unoccupied lightbulb socket,
licked her index finger to test its voltage –
    bingo balls halted and the whole hall gasped
        in darkness.

Grey plaits and a stutter
meant she was homeschooled, kept indoors,
    but I still see Kimberley singing when I look
        in mirrors behind bottles of spirits.

Insect Eucharist

They deafened
the flies when they tried
to clap them dead.

All afternoon,
observed from a spider's-
eye view, concussed

bluebottles flew
into the hard glass surface
of escape

and crash-landed
on the windowsill. Toppling
a rocking chair

they clambered
over furniture to swat
a daddy-long-legs,

pinching its limbs
until they laid limp like
strands of hair.

Earwigs choking
under an avalanche
of dirt and lint

in the hoover
bag were lucky not to
hear a ladybird's

body pop
between a finger and
thumb, mummified

in toilet paper
and buried at sea with
one flush.

The gossamer
that garlanded the ceiling
was torn down

when it turned
dark and they sellotaped
the letterbox

and sealed
the doors with draught excluders.
But one moth

hidden in a keyhole
flapped dust from its wings,
floated into an open

mouth to place
itself on the sleeping tongue
for communion.

Glass bottom boat

Neither sea-sickness nor curfew swayed me
worming through the rectangled crowd;
their faces scaly and Bridlington blue.
Rogue elbows and wrecking-ball breasts
knocked any question out of me reaching the front
where I swear I saw a mermaid nursing her
lover's skeleton, still wearing flippers,
goggles and snorkel.

No one stopped me vaulting the barrier
but when I started stamping on the glass platform
adult hands hooked my oxters
reeling me in, kicking and flailing
before I broke through.
Afterwards, curled up in a pile of coats,
my mother peeled back my ears to reveal
the gills I had drawn with her eye-liner
pencil.

Sisters of Highbury

1.

All the best trains
travel north, I thought
when the eldest bought
me a donkey jacket;
the men in the Miners'
Welfare called me
Michael Foot
of the climbing frames
and I tied knots
in the previous
owner's handkerchiefs
for no memory
in particular then
threw them away before
filling the pockets
with sand from
the cement factory.
I kept an acorn warm
as ordered but dropped
it during her nervous
breakdown; she said her
face felt numb and
there were spiders
in the soup but
I explained they were
croutons and cried
like a tilted candle
in the other room
when the doctor
put her to sleep
for an afternoon.

2.

All the best trains
travel south, I wrote
in a letter to
the youngest the week
before she met me
at Kings Cross.
Every night
I sleepwalked
down the corridor
outside their bedsit
where they cooked me
carpet picnics on
a Baby Belling.
She showed me
cathedrals of comic
books and arcades
(and didn't lie about
Soho) and adult-high
toys – someone said
I was the most
doleful boy in Hamley's
the day I went home.

3.

One married an Arab
with golden slippers,
the other flew away
to Florida to paint.
Then the cat-fights began
and I would dab
their scratches with
cotton buds and antiseptic.
Their exchanges are so
cold their breath
makes mist.
Both still dote on me
despite us having
different fathers and
I feel lower than
Cain knowing I talked
one into an abortion
and wasn't there for
the other when she
miscarried twins.

Between the slide and library

Flakes of paint, shedding from the Kenning Park gate frame,
showered a pigtail-topped toddler and her grandfather
with rust-dusted charcoal confetti.
The sun seared his skin, sulking on his joints
like rag-doll cotton and he regretted wearing a cardigan –
among other things.

Wringing dungaree straps and creasing her face at the wind,
the child tumbled towards the seesaw for balance.
Splashes of sunlight bouncing off the slide blinded her,
as she mewed back to her grandfather wheezing by the
    library;
one arm draped over his paunch, waving with his other.
Fingers at half-mast.

Once saddled in the swing, he creaked after her.
She flailed and jutted to propel herself forward
and he yanked his collar, feeling sweat chain-link his fringe.
Two steps and humid thunder rolled upwards from his
    brogues
to the scratched tobacco tin in his breast pocket.
Roundabout's spin slowed.

Clawing for the slide steps, he sank backwards
and clattered to the grass – like a tired ironing board.
The child dismounted and stammered to her grandfather's
    side:
he had played dead before but was not so docile.
She tugged at the already-stretched wool; dribble on her lips,
dusk in his eyes.

Kissing the kerb

Clay Cross is still there. Epileptoidal town
tucked under the Peaks (Matlock and Ashover).
Alfreton and Chesterfield hold the handles
of a skipping rope while it hops in-between
singing the playground rhyme:
'My mother says you're a gypsy queen.'

Shop faces are shuttered on Sundays
and Wednesday afternoons along Market Street.
Planted daffodils droop in the mining memorial
coal cart, where High Street dips,
commemorating
the closure of Derby Road and Parkhouse Pit.

Turn the corner of Broadleys and housewives
take their wheelie-bins for a walk,
complaining about the doors being ripped
from the hinges of their gas meter cabinets.
Tipsy husbands, danger on their lips,
rinsing their fingers with vinegar
to wash off nicotine stains,
talk of boredom, doledom, doldrum –
now the pipeline factory has closed down.
There are jobs at the taxi firms if you own a car
and can stay sober long enough to drive one.

Children pester people to buy them cigarettes
outside Aerated Waters ice cream parlour;
they should be spending their pocket money
on knickerbocker glories.

And there's the kerb at the mouth of Slater's Yard.
Shin-high, two-tiered; three youths brutally
ending a school rivalry, dried blood smeared
on the concrete days after like damson jam.
Still, people stay there, craving the rough affection,
similar to how an owner will stoop to grovel
for a lick on the face from his dog
knowing it has used the same tongue
to clean its arsehole.

Supermarket Hill

Temporary fencing caged a legend
behind the Somerfield side of Market Street.
    Taller than the snail-brown tower
in the fire station yard, it was the town's rampart;
protecting its identity, casting shadows
    broad as Britain across the car park.

    In winter, truants wearing bin-liner cassocks
would penguin-slide to the bottom where icicles,
brittle as kitten ribs, trembled on blackberry bushes.

    Sledges slalomed between abandoned
shopping trolleys with the pound coins prized
    from the handlebar locks. Tonsils swelled
and hot aching hands packed snowballs with gravel
to launch at those shouting from the summit.

Summer holidays started, and without knowing
each others' names, boys picked sides to play army;
    a shirtless commando, all puppy fat
and inverted nipples, chased his bandage-helmet enemy
    who'd had his ridiculed ears pinned back.

When the sky turned to lemonade, aluminium cans
were foraged from cow parsley, tested with fridge magnets
    and traded at the Tip for tuck shop money.

    Now, signposts skirting scalped and flattened
ground say, in so many words, that
    the paperboy has nowhere to stash his left-over
        deliveries and tearaways wanting to kiss
their siblings' babysitter must look elsewhere.

Shopkeepers put pencils behind their ears,
and the junior school has been moved to make room
for a Tesco's. Still, for the time being,
everyone can see more of the outside world.

Three crucifixes

on a West Midlands hill
in a land horizontal as quarter-past-nine,
spotlit, casting plaid shadows
across the mansion behind –
how many Christs can be hammered
up and how many hot cross buns
can be choked down?

Hooded pilgrims wander the hard shoulder
tearing at speedwell
and threatening to pelt cyclists
with shovelled roadkill;
their bank holiday hopes exploded
beneath a Volvo's bonnet.

A resurrection away from recovery
they turn and smirk at the wooden triple Ts,
but would they poke fun
at a synagogue or Sikhs
parading the streets for Vaisakhi?

I was reminded of the Sunday hours
when a certain fear
was put into me,
when I held my breath as though
I was decanting a loved-one's ashes
into a fountain pen.

Hosanna to a hedgehog

Glass splashing in the bottle banks
behind The Walton Arms was the only sound heard
when she hungrily scurried from under
the spire-high conifers
overlooking a cat's cradle of washing lines.
Snout tapered and twitching, sniffing out a bowl filled with
forgotten
dog food propping open a porch door, she felt fleas
trickle through her spines but didn't care once meat
slithered about her teeth –
a welcomed change from crunching woodlice shells.

Startled by boys' voices, the cul-de-sac became unsafe
and she sat panting in televisual twilight flickering from
living room
windows. There was a space near St. Augustine's Church:
during the day children played there, waving shapes
in grey grit and scraping smiley faces in soil
with lollipop sticks.

But at night it was deserted and littered with soggy crisps
and biscuits.
A shed missing its bottommost planks provided a sawdusted
nest, and nearby an elderly couple left milk-soaked bread
on their doorstep for her (if the others didn't get there first).

Suddenly the ground beneath her small claws vanished
just a few paving stones into her pilgrimage. Molten saliva
dripped from fangs clamping her prickly hide, blunt
as knitting needles against a spaniel's soft lips.

Usually she was dropped after one bite. Instead she was
    carried
for three streets; past the church and its heaven-swept
    courtyard,
past the dentist's and the pebbledashed garages,
until she was discarded like a broken brush head on Jaw
    Bones Hill.
Headlamps roared by the tawny ball, curled up and tense
    with fright,
between the double yellow lines.

  Cats thrashing in a flowerbed
  signalled the end of her respite and she opened
her blackcurrant eyes to see something
resembling minced steak.
With muffled grunts, she tasted some
and swallowed, noticing where it came from – a flattened
    double
    of herself, crushed by rush hour, the innards
squeezed out through its mouth like toothpaste. Eviscerated.
She continued eating regardless, thinking
  in her spiky way: 'It's what they would've wanted.'

There, those men laugh at pigeons

for the patrons of East End Wines

Blinking one eye at a time, they huddle
together, wearing thin clothes even in winter,
shivering like fridges in the middle of the night.

They drip down steps and slopes under
a dual carriageway canopy, each welcomed
with candour spread into the corners,

waving to the woman with a square
patch of grey hair draped across her forehead
like she was wearing a dish cloth as a fascinator.

One of them introduced a dining chair bought
at a car boot sale, explaining the cardigan
thrown into the bargain was some grandmother's.

Such unnerving chuckles can be heard
in the falling feathers of bird strike, seeming
to be the final blow in a bloody pillow fight.

Rather than kicking up crisp leaves in autumn
they swing their scuffed loafers at
gingernut crumbs and soiled bandages in the gutter;

tufted heads a crawlspace for guilty thoughts,
listening to the Muhammadan arrow of sound
when a taxi driver speeds across the flyover.

Oyster-shell skin and every sentiment scavenged,
feeling their way through exhaust pipe miasma,
they emerge elated as breath through a harmonica.

Upon finding abandoned crutches in East End Park

Stranger items have been tripped over in the street,
but, one parched afternoon when blood was soup,
collapsed across the kerb, those traditional sticks
complete with rubber curls that sit under armpits
gave me such hope approaching the elbow of the hedge.
Turning left could be a Pentecostal preacher palming
a cripple's forehead or even Jesus himself
after a sermon on Ivy Mount, uttering to the leper:
                    'Be clean, be clean.'
Tiny Tim would be catching coins tossed from Velux
windows and blessing everyone in the working men's club.
There was a clacking of oak on concrete, seeing
a paraplegic dancing on wooden legs and a longjohnsilvered
Leodian cutlassing schoolchildren into the Aire
and Calder Navigation. No miracles or adventure rounding
the corner, though; just dusk and litter trickling
towards my house where I watch too much television.

Lonely birthdays

En guard, Armitage Shanks!
The toilet brush lunged and then holstered.
Wearing two jackets I checked the letterbox –
no postman yet.

Outside my apartment block
wind whipped in a cyclone of leaves and litter
and sucked thin white liners from rubbish bins
abutting benches.

I plodded through puddles
making the baking soda in my boots (an old
wives tale for freshening dank-smelling leather)
fizz between my toes.

Smeared police horse dung
halted commuters (holding half-opened umbrellas,
hanging upside-down like sleeping fruit bats)
on the zebra crossing.

I listened to incidental street music:
slurping plunger sounds when teenagers kiss,
the snare drum thud of a stifled sneeze,
and the busker's bum notes – I'll drink alone tonight
and die of a hangover in the morning.

Emotionally ransacked
I went home, rode the lift to my first floor flat
and pressed my eyes against the letterbox to find
it brimming with envelopes.

A search for permanence

Watching you roll cigarettes for my father
across the table in The Duck And Drake,
I probably had pimples on my chin, turning
newspaper pages: there was a boy allergic
to food, above seahorses found in the Thames.

You asked the landlord to mute
the television for the jukebox.
Beer mats pirouette and I tried
weaning myself off our pasts and
onto stout and pork scratchings
to broaden my scrawny torso.
Drunken bores, with throats that
can't be cleared, mourn Woolworths.
I doodle us as stickmen walking
up paths in the property section,
then spy on smokers outside who
can't see sky for patio umbrellas.
Addresses for each cold back
bedroom we've been crammed into
almost fill the crossword but
your chipped fingernail polish
blocks my biro – O what an honour
it is to peg your knickers out
to dry and sit in your bathwater.

A widower watches their home burn down

Misguided rioters wouldn't know
how many happy anniversary banners
had hung over the cloakroom door,
or that he kept the teal sheets
wrapped round them on their last night
in bed together, in the chest of drawers.

Revolutionary bells didn't ring
when, twenty-six years prior,
he brushed confetti off his lapels
during the registry office ceremony,
unaware that her bones would ache
with cancer the day they decided
to move to Tottenham.

Loot her jewellery and smash the vases
rather than firebomb the shop below
their flat; a thief wouldn't find
the biscuit barrel filled with letters
and ticket stubs in the kitchen
cupboard but the flames would.

Imagining their photo album melting
in the arson of his memories,
he closed his eyes, unable
to endure another cremation.

Injuries sustained after a demobbing

Sand and cumin wafted in
when he returned for Christmas.
The wife slung tinsel over
her man-mirage of a husband,
smudging war-paint
whilst kissing him welcome.
Children helped him remove
boots tangled in mile-long laces
and endless eyelets, then held out
crackers for their father to pull.
No bad jokes or paper crowns appeared
when the snap boomed
in his ears, shattering his hand
and splintering bone and
every stick of furniture.

Poised in Sunday League stripes,
he waited for the corner kick,
peeling away from players
in different colours standing guard
around the six-yard box.
The referee's whistle screamed
as he triggered a mine
buried beneath the penalty spot,
flinging his teammates
high over the goalposts.
No magic sponge or deep heat rub
could rescue his mangled foot
or stop the flow
of camouflage
bleeding from the stump.

Wind chimes, jangling like dog tags
woke him up before his sweat-
soaked pyjamas turned cold.
He shook desert from his head
and felt for a beret and epaulettes
finding only knotted shoulders
and matted hair.
A dream almost detonated
between the pillows
pressed to each temple;
he dived onto the bedside
table to smother an alarm clock's
final bleats, as streetlamps
shone where the sun
failed to rise in the east.

Where the stork won't land

Soberly, toast invaded neighbouring noses, steam rose
from grates outside as frozen sewage cracked below the
    street.
Remembrance silence engulfed the cemetery of houses to
    allow
her howls, rolling around the toilet bowl, to raise eyebrows.
Weak yet smiling she returned to bed and waited
for the fluoride in her glass of water to clear.
Pipes jerked, gaping yawns locked many jaws and a pair of
    overalls
stretched cruciform by his gatepost, finished
a trilogy of cigarettes stubbed out in a ramekin.

Already miserable prescriptions loitered outside the
    chemist's
halfway between the train depot and canal; all foreheads
corrugated, each face pockmarked like a dartboard;
their orchestral coughing in need of a conductor.
A high-pitched sneeze, abrupt as a cockerel, woke her –
the slump in the mattress beside her had left to retrieve
a newspaper. Feeling colour come back to her cheeks
she palpated her tumid belly, underneath the duvet,
sensing genesis was taking place.

Premature nativity

Narrow pavements forced him into the charity shop,
dank paperback and dirty china fouling the air,
somnolently (shirt and suit familiar as pyjamas)
searching through other lives, less bloody,
less biblical, giddy – like the life cycle
of frog ornaments shelved near the till
or the swallows arrowing across an oriental parasol,
leaning unopened, bamboo spokes
poking through the paper.

Out he walked, five minutes later, wearing
a woollen tie, a collection of novellas holstered
in his pocket, clutching a porcelain tortoise
with a bobbing head and limbs –
each used item negating new grief,
one a gift for a person nurturing another.

Mothers sleep but milk still comes

Afternoons cartwheel, flashing midnight's knickers at me,
left over from supper with a headache of dead flowers
(mulch for our suburb) and a future waiting upstairs.

Threadbare ewes rub their mutton against gateposts
after a bachelor wearing a bag of dye blots them with love.

Suede impervious to spear thistle, the bullock bellows
waking himself from a castrated fantasy, labours to give
    chase
teased by uddersway, but collapses, gnats fizzing above his
    rump.

The iron-clad stream bleeds into Lancashire
and intravenously feeds the house for hire with soft water.

Here farmers' sons washed windblush and dung from their
    faces
then, handsome as horseshoes, they'd call Goldilocks a tart
for jumping into three different beds (the mother tuts).

From my throne on onion-skin-weathered stone
I can see backcombed goosegrass and the Church of St
    Someone.

Abide with the vicar walking mufti before service
and he will point out the pauper's grave where, centuries ago,
a drunk congregation lowered the coffin lopsided.

The spilled corpse, laid to rest outside of its case,
suffered the impact from the pat of the spade.

Pulling at wool caught on barbed wire – like God's beard –
reminds me these aren't fields or a perimeter
that stops us from strolling into Gomorrah or Morecambe.

Lonelier than a leap year, away from the rowdy guests
I look out again, suckling at the scenery, feeding off the
     future.

On waving to a family behind glass

Billiard balls are easier to swallow
than the dread clogging my throat
when my wife lifted our son
to the front door window to say goodbye.
Not quite pressing a hand against
carriage glass on a train to Belsen
or blowing kisses inside a space helmet
before boarding the Challenger shuttle,
nevertheless I felt my chest tighten
at the sight, like clay setting in a kiln.
The imagined farewell at the end
of Ranby Prison visiting hours
and halfway house in *Cathy Come Home*
tugged at my bottom lip, even though
I would return from work in less than
what is deemed a good night's sleep,
a day closer to retirement.

Eden on a teatray

No more will coat-hangers crucify these work shirts –
they will always be worn whilst turning over the allotment
    with a fork.
Long gone are the doilies and carriage clock-kept lives,
the oil-clothed shelves and house devalued by disowned
    children
        and empty wedding vows.

Selling all the furniture (save a truckle bed) covered the costs
of the rotavator, leek tunnel and felt on the shed roof
and put an end to cerebral clutter and the scraping of chairs.
Handing over the rent-book brought forward the thought of
    living
        next to a childhood haunt:

Blood Wood was an open-air abattoir where Victorian
    butchers
would slaughter pigs and trade other livestock that they'd gut,
tossing the ropes of muscle into leaves to make them lighter
    in transit.
For us truants it was a firing range for air riflemen
and cheese knife slingers, wounding bark with 22. calibre
    pellets
and kitchen utensils. Look away when best friends squat
    behind brambles
wiping their arses on dockleaves, nettles stinging their thighs.
Trying to plug these whippersnappered memories is
    impossible;
the fingers on lips, the never-to-tell – better to believe
in an ornamental horserace when a mother is thrown
    against

a mantelpiece. The Baptist's wife explained my namesake
('you are 'the gift' in Hebrew and a disciple') then cleared
    the teacups
and biscuits and told me to build a paradise with topsoil
    and twigs.

Everyone here envies the scarecrows; nothing to do but watch
husks break, not a straw-stuffed counterpart to waltz or
    spar with.
Out of all those lonely nights it was the sound of a panicked
    rabbit doe
killing her kittens in fright during a thunderstorm which
        made me clutch my quilt.

Splinterpricks and rough thumbprints are the gardener's
    stigmata;
and they say I am old now, and look like an owl without
    feathers,
false teeth loose on my gums, demijohns of homebrewed
    wine
keep me company, listening to life level out to a hum
        like communal prayer.

The Wendy House

Now that the streetlamps have stolen the stars
from the afternoon sky, sleep, content
and lovely as custard, pours over us. We sit
with winter on the settee, arm in arm –
our legs interlaced like denim snakes,
bedlam pressed between our palms.

The boiler bubbles and hisses, pumping tea
into the radiators; a roman candle
bursts inside the fireplace when it's poked.
We watch a carpet waterfall tumbling
down the stairs to the living room, where cigarettes
are kissed rather than smoked.

Outside, beyond our back garden, the farmer is growing
    snow;
his brown eiderdown has been overrun with marshmallow,
    and the clouds
have split and spilt talcum powder on the hills around.

The cast of breakfast waits to tread a toast stage;
mackerel paddle in the blue waves of the grill
and ghostly poached eggs haunt the saucepan.
Yolks explode and a red button is clicked
to start a hurricane in the kettle.

Because warmth passes through the terrace walls,
each tenant is snug as hands in pockets. Our jumpers
and sweaters stop wrestling in the washing machine
when the suds begin to drown;
so we lasso the clothes horse, unfold it
and hang our insides out.

More than circumstance in common

Shivering infant in the swimming baths
we'll have you home before long,
back to your nursery with circus wallpaper,
muffled in cellular wool.

Like a miniature Houdini, you wriggle free
of any burden on your shoulders –
unlike the nearly-man holding you afloat
in the shallow end.

Once you're reared, these mollycoddled mornings,
soothed and swaddled in honesty,
will be forgotten, but there's a double helix
that twists in both our blood;

standing up for bastards.
Midlands sinew will grip
the hands you shake, the thighs you clasp
in the bunker of adulthood.

Towelled together I feel
your delicate unfettered breath on my neck
like gale force wind through a keyhole,
an uncertain murmur, not quite a gurgle,
but the first mouthing fumble for father.